Something's <u>Different</u>
About Andrew

Written and Illustrated by
Kyndal Gary

Something's Different About Andrew
Written and Illustrated by
Kyndal Gary

Publishing Assistance
Sue Breeding
Creating-Design
P.O. Box 1785
Columbus, IN 47202

www.creating-design.com

Something's Different About Andrew

Written and Illustrated by
Kyndal Gary

This is Andrew.

Andrew is very different from
everyone else, which is good.

Why is he different from everyone else?

Because Andrew has Autism,
something he didn't know he had.

Andrew was interested in dinosaurs.

He would have toys and books about dinosaurs.

Because of his Autism, he knew
everything about dinosaurs.

But Andrew didn't like certain sounds, especially loud sounds.

He was sensitive to lights and he had trouble speaking eye-to-eye with others.

Some of the boys at school were not so nice to Andrew.

"Hey, Weirdo," one of them said. "Are you stupid, or were you just born like that?"

The other boys laughed, and this made
Andrew feel small.

Some of the girls in school were not as nice.

"You dummy," one of them yelled. "Can't you do anything right? This is why nobody likes you!"

One of the girls laughed, and this made
Andrew feel even worse.

One day after school, Andrew went back home and asked his mother, "Mom, is there something wrong with me?"

She was surprised that Andrew would ask that question.

"Of course not," she said to him. "You have something called Autism."

Andrew still didn't know what Autism was.

"What's Autism?" he finally asked.

"Autism is when someone has trouble communicating or interacting with others," said Andrew's mom. "And people with it are also sensitive to lights and sounds."

"But your Autism is also very special, too," said Andrew's mom. "Like how you're focused on dinosaurs and how you're very smart."

With a confident smile, Andrew began to understand. "Thank you, Mom," he said.

From that day on, Andrew went to a special group of kids who also had Autism. With the help of Mrs. Daugherty, he learned how to speak to others.

One day, the same bullies came to hurt Andrew.

"Hey, Weirdo, where are you going?" One boy asked.

"Come back, you dummy!" The girl yelled.

But he wasn't listening.

Andrew even made a new friend.

"Hello, I'm Andrew," he said with a smile.

A Word From Kyndal Gary

Autism is a wide spectrum, which explains how people with it function. My type of Autism is high functioning, which helps me be more social and self-sufficient. However, other levels of Autism affect other people's social skills and ability to be self-sufficient. Some would fidget, scream, or slobber, and would need certain vest and support from others.

People with severe Autism are in need of help and care. But this doesn't mean they're not people. I believe people with less-severe Autism are uniquely gifted. Those who have it severely, I believe are still unique and wonderfully made people.

If there are people out there who laugh and make fun of others' differences, they definitely need a change of heart. For everyone out there with other disorders and disabilities, I want to say you are special human beings, and are created for a purpose. God bless you.

This Book Belongs To

70264664R00015

Made in the USA
Middletown, DE
12 April 2018